DEDICATION

This book is dedicated to my mother,
LaVerne Marie Onstad
who encouraged me to write at a very early age.

Tommy built a tree house.
It wasn't very hard.
His daddy helped him build it,
right in his backyard.

They built it in an apple tree.
They built it way up high.
When Tom looks out the window,
he can see the birds fly by.

The tree house
has two windows,
a sunroof and a door.
There are curtains
on the windows
and a carpet on the floor.

When Tommy's
friends come over
they always like to play.
Up in Tommy's tree house
they pass the time away.

They talk and play
their little games
on long hot summer nights.
Except for little Jimmy.
He's afraid of heights!

All the others know that
when Jimmy comes around,
Jimmy always spends his time
playing on the ground.

So Tommy held a meeting
with Stan and Kate and Timmy,
to figure out exactly
what they could do
for little Jimmy.

They wanted little Jimmy
to share in all their fun
and little Jimmy wanted
to play with everyone.

After several hours
Tom, Kate, Tim and Stan
put their heads together
and came up with a plan.

They all told little Jimmy
not to be afraid.
He'd never overcome his fears
if on the ground he stayed.

Little Jimmy thought
it through
and realized they were right.
He knew he must go up there
to overcome his fright.

So up the wooden ladder
carefully he climbed.
He put aside his worries
and left them all behind.

When little Jimmy
reached the door
he slowly climbed inside.
His friends congratulated him
and Jimmy beamed with pride.

He was happy that he overcame
his awful fear of heights
and now he can
share in their fun
on long hot summer nights.

So if you have a worry,
like little Jimmy had,
try to overcome it.
It can't be all that bad.

Try to face your problems
and set aside your fears.
You'll be happy
that you did
throughout the
coming years.

Made in the USA
San Bernardino, CA
18 July 2018